DISEASE
UPDATE

The Flu and Pneumonia Update

Alvin and Virginia Silverstein and Laura Silverstein Nunn

Enslow Publishers, Inc.

40 Industrial Road	PO Box 38
Box 398	Aldershot
Berkeley Heights, NJ 07922	Hants GU12 6BP
USA	UK

http://www.enslow.com

Acknowledgments

The authors thank Gary Maltz, M.D., and Laura Rees Willett, M.D., for their many helpful comments and suggestions.

Library of Congress Cataloging-in-Publication Data

Silverstein, Alvin.
    The flu and pneumonia update / Alvin and Virginia Silverstein,
and Laura Silverstein Nunn.—1st ed.
       p. cm. — (Disease update)
    Includes bibliographical references and index.
    ISBN 0-7660-2480-6 (hardcover)
    1. Influenza—Juvenile literature. 2. Pneumonia—Juvenile literature.
I. Silverstein, Virginia B. II. Nunn, Laura Silverstein. III. Title. IV. Series.
RC150.S47 2005
616.2'03-dc22

                  2005005988

Printed in the United States of America

10 9 8 7 6 5 4 3 2 1

To Our Readers:
We have done our best to make sure all Internet Addresses in this book were active and appropriate when we went to press. However, the author and the publisher have no control over and assume no liability for the material available on those Internet sites or on other Web sites they may link to. Any comments or suggestions can be sent by e-mail to comments@enslow.com or to the address on the back cover.

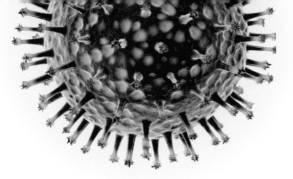

Contents

Flu and Pneumonia

What is it?

Flu: a highly contagious disease caused by an influenza virus.

Pneumonia: a serious disease in which the lungs become filled with fluid.

Who gets it?

All ages, all races, both sexes; most dangerous to the elderly, young children, and people with health problems.

How do you get it?

Flu: mainly by breathing virus-contaminated droplets; also by touching virus-contaminated people or objects, then touching one's eyes or nose.

Pneumonia: infections by bacteria, viruses, or fungi; or inhaling certain chemicals in food particles, liquids, gases, or dust.

What are the symptoms?

Flu: headaches, chills, muscle aches, coughing, sore throat, and fever.

Pneumonia: chills, severe chest pain, coughing, high fever, tiredness, and difficulty breathing.

How is it treated?

Flu: resting, drinking plenty of liquids, and taking medications such as ibuprofen and cough syrup for symptoms. People at high risk for complications can take antiviral medications, such as Tamiflu or Relenza.

Pneumonia: taking antibiotics or antiviral drugs; oxygen given through a breathing mask or respirator may be used to aid breathing.

How can it be prevented?

Flu: vaccines, especially for people most at risk for complications. Frequent hand washing can help prevent the spread of flu viruses.

Pneumonia: vaccines protect against bacterial pneumonia. Avoiding close contact with people who have the flu, washing hands regularly, and keeping the body strong by practicing good health habits can help prevent infection.

New Jersey Nets' forward Kenyon Martin shoots over his opponent during Game 4 of the 2003 NBA finals. Although Martin had a sore throat and a cough, he did not find out he had the flu until the next day. By Game 5, he was having a very hard time on the court.

1

Flu Season

IN 2003, THE NEW JERSEY NETS basketball team made the NBA finals for the second year in a row. This time they were determined to win. It looked like they had a good chance. Going into Game 4, they were trailing the San Antonio Spurs two games to one, but they were battling back. Kenyon Martin, the Nets' star forward, seemed to be his usual enthusiastic self, firing up the home crowd as well as his teammates. Nobody would have guessed that he really wasn't feeling up to par. When he woke up that morning, Martin's throat was sore. He was tired and had a headache. Was he getting a cold? He couldn't be sick! His team needed him. As the day went on, Martin started coughing.

Sometimes he felt hot, and then suddenly he was shivering with a chill. When the game started, he tried not to let whatever "bug" he had affect his play. Amazingly, he scored twenty points, and the Nets' win tied up the series two games apiece.

The next day, "K-Mart," as his teammates like to call him, felt even worse. But he showed up for practice anyway. At this point it was obvious that Martin was ill, so his coach had him checked out by the team's medical staff. They told him that this was not just a bad cold, as Martin thought. He had the flu, and they told him to go home and get some rest.

Game 5 took place on Friday the 13th, which turned out to be an unlucky day for Kenyon Martin and the New Jersey Nets. Martin was determined to play even though he was obviously run down. He had a really tough time on the court, scoring only four points and committing four turnovers that led to important scoring by the other team. Martin's teammates did everything they could to help him. But it wasn't enough. The Nets lost to the Spurs 93–83. Now trailing in the series, the Nets were disappointed, but they had hopes that Martin would feel better for Game 6. "I think if he gets a little rest, he'll be ready [on Sunday]," coach

Byron Scott told the press.[1] But that did not happen. Martin was still struggling with the flu in Game 6, and made only 3 of his 23 shots that night. The Nets were unable to pull it off and lost to the Spurs 88–77, which ended their chances of winning the NBA championship.[2]

The flu, short for *influenza,* can strike anyone, even someone who is strong, healthy, and athletic like Kenyon Martin. When the flu hits, it hits hard, and the symptoms can last for a week or two. Instead of running

> **Every year, more than 25 million people in the United States come down with the flu during "flu season."**

around the court and wearing himself out, Kenyon should have been getting plenty of rest in bed.

Though people sometimes confuse the common cold with the flu, the two illnesses feel very different. A cold typically starts out with perhaps a sore throat, then gradually develops into a runny or stuffy nose, along with sneezing or coughing. Flu feels a lot worse.

It usually comes on suddenly and packs a powerful punch with a high fever, headache, coughing, extreme tiredness and weakness, and serious aches and pains. It is also a much more dangerous illness. It makes the body so weak that some people become vulnerable to other illnesses, such as bronchitis (infection of the breathing tubes) and pneumonia (infection of the lungs), which can be life threatening.

Flu is caused by an influenza virus, and like a cold, it is very contagious—it can spread easily from person to person. Every year, more than 25 million people in the United States come down with the flu during "flu season," which generally occurs from November through March.[3] (Kenyon Martin's case was unusual because it occurred in June. Some doctors say that many cases of "summer flu" are actually caused by some other, flu-like, virus.)

There are several kinds, or "strains," of flu viruses, and they are constantly changing. The flu that is "going around" one year is likely to be somewhat different from the ones that were circulating the year before. Having the flu provides protection against catching that particular kind of flu virus again, and vaccines can be used to protect people from one or more flu strains.

But unless large numbers of people are protected against the current strains of flu viruses, the disease may spread widely, becoming an epidemic. Some years the natural changes in the flu viruses may lead to more dangerous forms, which are more likely to kill people. In 1918, a combination of circumstances led to the most serious and widespread flu epidemic in world history. Troop movements at the end of World War I helped to spread the germ, and meanwhile, the flu virus had changed into a particularly contagious and deadly form. Millions of people all over the world died. Fortunately, the flu epidemics that have occurred since then have not been as widespread or deadly. With the vaccines and treatments available in the twenty-first century, doctors hope that the world will never again have to face a nightmare like the great flu epidemic of 1918.

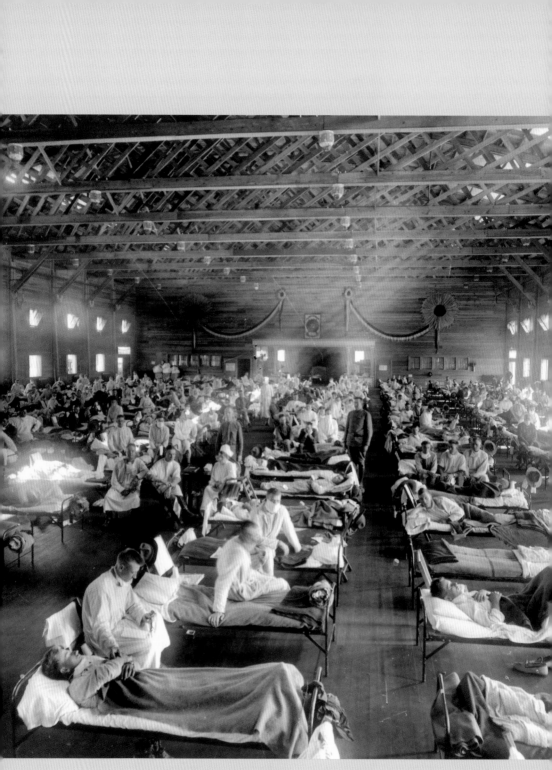

The influenza ward at Fort Riley, Kansas, in 1918.

2

Flu's Impact on History

THE WORST FLU EPIDEMIC in history happened in 1918 as a four-year battle between world powers was ending. World War I was brutal, killing nearly 10 million people. What no one ever expected, however, was the arrival of a new enemy—influenza. Normally easy to overcome, this form of influenza was vicious and deadly, killing more people in a single year than World War I had all together.

It all started in the United States, in an army camp at Fort Riley, Kansas. Weather conditions there were tough on the soldiers, with the bitter cold winters and sweltering summers, as well as the blinding dust storms. Even more unbearable was the stench from the mounds of manure produced by the horses. Burning the manure was the quickest and easiest method of getting rid of it. On March 9, 1918, as tons of horse manure were being burned, a severe dust storm forced everyone to take cover. The whipping dust, together with the ash from the burning manure, turned the skies into a stinky dark haze.

Two days later, on March 11, army cook Albert Gitchell woke up with a terrible headache, a severe sore throat, and muscle aches all over his body. Gitchell left his barracks and headed for the camp hospital. When he got there, the sergeant on duty took his temperature, which was 103 degrees, and asked Gitchell to describe his symptoms. Gitchell was placed in isolation just in case he was contagious. Soon Corporal Lee W. Drake came to the infirmary, complaining of symptoms similar to Gitchell's. By noon, over 100 soldiers had come down with the same illness. By the end of the week, more than 500 men at the camp were sick. Soon other overcrowded military camps were also struck. At Fort Riley, forty-six men died, but the army did not let medical problems interfere with the war efforts. Men were shipped overseas in crowded conditions, and with them they carried influenza.

By that fall, the soldiers had carried the flu to France—and it had become much worse. Before, the disease was contagious but not very deadly. Now symptoms had become more serious, including dizziness, vomiting, sweating, and difficulty breathing. Soon many influenza patients developed a vicious form of pneumonia. Large numbers of people started to die, often rather quickly and with serious

> No one is sure exactly how many people died in the 1918 flu epidemic, but estimates range from 20 million up to 40 million people worldwide.

lung damage. The second wave of the flu spread from France to England and then to Spain, where it killed 8 million people and acquired the popular name of Spanish flu (even though the disease did not originate there). The Spanish flu spread eastward to the army in Germany, then to Russia, China, Japan, and down to South Africa, across to India, and then to South America.

In the United States, the flu was at first confined to the army, but in early September 1918, the first civilian case was reported in Boston. The disease spread quickly. By the end of September ten thousand Americans had died. Poor sanitary conditions and the scarcity of doctors and nurses (many of whom were serving in the

EXCESS MORTALITY in U·S·CITIES DURING INFLUENZA EPIDEMIC

PERCENT OF POPULATION DYING

CITY	1918–1919			
	SEPT. 8–NOV. 23 10 WEEKS	NOV. 24–FEB. 1 10 WEEKS	FEB. 2 – MAR 29 8 WEEKS	TOTAL 28 WEEKS
PHILADELPHIA	.69	.01	.03	.73
FALL RIVER	.59	.05	.04	.68
PITTSBURGH	.59	.12	.06	.77
BALTIMORE	.57	.03	.0	.60
SYRACUSE	.55	.02	.02	.58
NASHVILLE	.55	.16	.12	.83
BOSTON	.50	.12	.0	.62
NEW HAVEN	.49	.13	.0	.61
NEW ORLEANS	.49	.21	.0	.71
ALBANY	.48	.03	.02	.53
BUFFALO	.47	.10	.04	.61
WASHINGTON	.45	.12	.0	.54
LOWELL	.44	.10	.03	.56
SAN FRANCISCO	.42	.31	.02	.74
CAMBRIDGE	.39	.12	.0	.50
NEWARK	.38	.11	.04	.53
PROVIDENCE	.38	.13	.03	.53
RICHMOND	.35	.18	.02	.55
DAYTON	.33	.02	.03	.37
OAKLAND	.33	.22	.01	.56
CHICAGO	.32	.09	.04	.46
NEW YORK	.30	.09	.08	.47
CLEVELAND	.27	.11	.04	.42
LOS ANGELES	.27	.26	.01	.55
MEMPHIS	.25	.02	.09	.37
ROCHESTER	.25	.12	.03	.40
KANSAS CITY	.25	.27	.08	.60
DENVER	.24	.32	.07	.63
CINCINNATI	.22	.13	.11	.46
OMAHA	.22	.20	.0	.43
LOUISVILLE	.19	.04	.14	.37
ST. PAUL	.19	.13	.02	.34
COLUMBUS	.19	.15	.07	.41
PORTLAND	.18	.22	.03	.42
TOLEDO	.17	.02	.0	.17
MINNEAPOLIS	.17	.11	.07	.24
SEATTLE	.16	.18	.02	.36
INDIANAPOLIS	.15	.09	.08	.31
BIRMINGHAM	.15	.15	.0	.29
MILWAUKEE	.15	.18	.03	.37
ST. LOUIS	.12	.18	.04	.34
SPOKANE	.11	.13	.02	.25
ATLANTA	.07	.13	.0	.19
GRAND RAPIDS	.04	.12	.04	.19

People in the cities across America died of the flu in 1918 and 1919. This chart shows the percent of the population that died in many cities between September 8, 1918 and March 29, 1919.

war effort) helped the epidemic to spread quickly. By the end of 1918, three hundred thousand Americans had died. A third wave of flu swept the world after the end of the war, but ended abruptly in the spring of 1919. By then the U.S. death toll had reached half a million. No one is sure exactly how many people died of the flu worldwide during that time, but estimates range from 20 million up to 40 million people. This was classified as a pandemic—an infectious disease that spreads all around the world, involving millions of people.[1]

Living in 1918

Imagine living in 1918 during the flu pandemic. Health officials were desperate to try to stop the spread of disease. They advised everyone to get plenty of rest, eat regularly, and "beware of persons shaking hands."[2] People were given hefty fines for spitting, sneezing, or coughing in public without a handkerchief.

Phone booths were boarded up, and dance halls, pool rooms, movie houses, libraries, ice cream parlors, churches, and saloons were closed. Some baseball players wore protective masks during their games. In Prescott, Arizona, a person who shook hands could be thrown in jail. At a West Coast naval base, drinking fountains were blowtorched every hour to sanitize them, phones were cleaned with alcohol, and guards were ordered to shoot to kill anyone who came or went without permission.[3]

Generally speaking, influenza is especially dangerous to the elderly and those who are already sick. But in 1918, an unusual mutation, or change, in the flu virus occurred that caused the organism to target normally healthy adults, many of whom were between twenty and forty years old.

Identifying the Flu Virus

Until 1918, scientists thought that influenza was caused by bacteria, since electron microscopes that would let them see viruses had not yet been invented. Viruses *could* be detected, however, by using a filter with holes so tiny that only viruses could fit through. In the 1890s, German scientist Richard Pfeiffer claimed that he had identified the culprit that causes influenza—a rod-shaped bacterium called *Haemophilus influenzae*. However, further studies showed that this bacterium was not always present in people with influenza.

During the 1918 pandemic, J. S. Koen, a veterinarian of the U.S. Bureau of Animal Industry in Iowa, noticed that a disease in pigs resembled the Spanish flu. He noted that in places where pigs and people lived close together, an outbreak in the family would be followed by an outbreak among the pigs, or vice versa. He

What Is a Bacterium?

A bacterium is a very tiny organism, too small to see without a microscope. It is made up of just a single cell. Some bacteria can live on their own, but others must depend on another organism—their host—for food and living space. Some bacteria harm their host, stealing nutrients and producing poisons. We call harmful bacteria "germs" and say that they cause diseases.

Haemophilus influenzae bacteria

believed that "swine flu," as he called it, and human influenza were actually the same illness, and that the pigs got the disease from humans. Koen's observation was largely ignored until a new discovery in 1931. Richard Shope, a pathologist from Princeton, New Jersey, passed mucus from sick pigs through a filter and then placed it in the noses of healthy pigs. The filter screened out any bacteria that might be present, leaving only viruses in the mucus. When the pigs became ill, he had proved that swine flu was spread by a virus.

Some historians have suggested that the 1918 flu pandemic may have started when the horse manure was burned at Fort Riley and breathed in by the soldiers. Research has shown that a number of animals,

What Is a Virus?

Viruses are much smaller than bacteria—so tiny that they can be seen only with a powerful electron microscope. Some look like balls with spikes sticking out all over. Others look like loaves of bread, coiled springs, or even tadpoles. Viruses depend on hosts to live, grow, and reproduce. They invade body cells and turn them into virus-making factories. When a cell is full of viruses, it bursts open, and hundreds of new viruses spill out. Each new virus finds a cell to invade and continues the process. Soon there are millions of viruses in a body—and the person feels miserable.

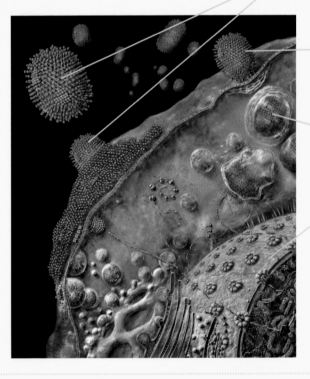

New viruses burst out of cell.

Virus lands on surface of cell.

Virus is inside cell.

Nucleus of cell makes copies of virus' genetic information; new viruses are made.

including birds, pigs, and horses, can carry the influenza virus. Sometimes the virus may spread to another species. For instance, it may jump

> Researchers ultimately discovered that there are three different types of viruses that can cause flu in humans.

from birds to pigs or horses, and then to humans. The virus, which thrives in the digestive tract, can be found in the animals' feces. It is possible, then, that the horse manure at Fort Riley was infected with the influenza virus, and when it was burned, the soldiers breathed in the contaminated dust and ash mixture.

In 1933, British researchers Wilson Smith, Christopher Andrewes, and Patrick P. Laidlaw were the first to identify the human flu virus. The researchers experimented on ferrets, hoping to be able to infect them with human influenza. They placed drops of fluid taken from the throats of human influenza patients into the noses of ferrets. After a couple of days, the animals were soon suffering from fever, sneezing, and runny noses, just like human flu victims.

Researchers ultimately discovered that there are three different types of viruses that can cause flu in humans. The one studied by the British team, as well as by Thomas Francis, was named influenza A. During the

Why Ferrets?

Ferrets, relatives of weasels, are not typical lab animals. Smith, Andrewes, and Laidlaw chose to work with them because these animals are very susceptible to canine distemper, a disease of dogs with symptoms similar to flu symptoms. The researchers thought that the germ causing flu might be related to the distemper virus. They were mistaken, but ferrets also turned out to be very susceptible to human influenza. After their experimental ferrets were infected with fluid from the throats of human patients, a lucky accident allowed the researchers to take the study a step further. One of the sick ferrets sneezed in Wilson Smith's face, and Smith promptly came down with the flu. The team used fluid from his throat, filtered to remove bacteria, to infect healthy ferrets. They also found that healthy ferrets caught the flu when they were placed in the same cage with sick ones.[4]

1940s, influenza B and then influenza C were discovered.

Influenza A is the type that causes pandemics. The most dangerous kind, it is also found in many animals, such as birds, horses, seals, swine, and whales. Influenza B and C are usually found only in humans. Influenza A and B produce very similar symptoms, but influenza B causes less severe epidemics and affects mainly children. Influenza C rarely causes illness.

Controlling the Flu

Researchers continued to study the influenza virus and worked hard to find a way to control the disease. In 1944, the first flu vaccine was developed by Thomas Francis and Jonas Salk (who later developed the polio vaccine). At the time, the vaccine was used primarily to protect soldiers in World War II, to keep the disease from spreading to the extent it had in 1918. The vaccine was made from a weakened virus, meaning that it could not cause an infection. However, the vaccine did produce side effects, such as fever and headaches. (Better

Thomas Francis (left) and Jonas Salk developed the first flu vaccine in 1944. They are shown here at a press conference in 1955 following the invention of the polio vaccine.

techniques have reduced the chances for side effects in today's flu vaccines.)

When the Asian flu epidemic came to the United States in 1957–1958, flu vaccines and increased education helped to keep the death toll down. Even though as many as seventy thousand Americans died, many people thought that it could have been a lot worse.

The next big U.S. outbreak was the Hong Kong flu, which occurred in 1968. Again, doctors offered flu vaccines and information on prevention. This time, only about 34,000 people died in the United States.[5] Populations have increased greatly since that time, and yet today, the annual death toll from flu in the United States is about 36,000 people.[6]

The World Health Organization (WHO) has been monitoring influenza viruses since 1947. More than two hundred influenza centers worldwide send virus samples from their patients to WHO centers in London, England; Melbourne, Australia; or Atlanta, Georgia. Viruses are tested there and given a name, which includes the virus type and the place it is from. This is how virus strains come to be known by popular names such as Hong Kong flu or Shanghai flu.

3

What Is the Flu?

DONNA HAD BEEN STAYING UP late all week studying for her college midterms. One night, near the end of the week, she developed a really bad headache, and she was feeling especially tired. She figured she was probably just worn out from all the studying she had been doing, so she closed her textbooks and decided to go to bed early. She hoped that, with some well-needed rest, she would feel better in the morning.

The next morning, Donna did not feel better. In fact, she was *much* worse. Her throat felt like it was on fire and her muscles ached all over. She could hardly get out of bed. She felt hot and sweaty, and then suddenly she got chills, and her body could not stop shaking. This was no time to be sick, she thought. She had two midterms that day.

Donna dragged herself to the health clinic on campus. Maybe they could give her something to make her feel better. There the nurse on duty took Donna's temperature. It was 104 degrees. After Donna described her symptoms, the nurse knew right away—she had the flu. Apparently, it was going around. Donna was the eighth student that week who had come into the health office with flu symptoms.

In most cases, flu is *not* fatal; it is just enough to make a person miserable for a week or two.

The nurse told Donna that the best thing to do was to stay in bed and drink plenty of fluids. An over-the-counter pain reliever would help relieve the aches and pains and bring down the fever. Donna should take it easy, and no, it was definitely not a good idea to take those two midterm exams that day! Not only would she be unable to concentrate, but she would be exposing all of her classmates to flu germs. She should also watch for any additional symptoms, such as breathing problems, which could be a sign of complications.

When Donna got back to the dorm, she left phone messages for her professors explaining that she had the flu and asking to arrange for makeup exams. As the day went on, she felt even sicker, with hardly enough energy to get herself a glass of juice or warm up some soup. Finally she called home and asked her parents to pick her up. She wound up missing a whole week of classes, but she was fully recovered by the time she got back to school.[1]

These days, the word *flu* does not conjure up images of death and destruction as it did in the days before flu vaccines and education on flu prevention were available. In most cases, flu is *not* fatal; it is just enough to make a person miserable for a week or two. By following some basic instructions, such as getting plenty of rest, drinking fluids, and taking over-the-counter medicines for symptoms, most people are usually back on their feet in a short time. But sometimes flu can be dangerous, especially for the elderly and people with other health conditions, such as asthma or heart problems. Even normally healthy people can develop complications from the flu when they do not follow the proper treatment, though this is rare.

The Flu Bug

The flu, or influenza (its medical name), is an infection of the respiratory system (the breathing passages and lungs) that is caused mainly by two kinds of influenza viruses, type A and type B. The virus can spread when an infected person coughs, sneezes, or even talks. This sends contaminated droplets into the air, which may be breathed in by nearby people. People can also pick up these viruses through hand contact or by touching the same object, such as a doorknob or telephone, and then

When an infected person sneezes, she can send flu-contaminated droplets into the air.

Flu on an Airplane

When you are flying on an airplane, you are breathing in the air that other passengers breathed out. The air inside a plane in flight is constantly being recycled. Filters and other treatments help to clean out germs, but sometimes they are not good enough. Airplanes are notorious for spreading contagious diseases. In a classic case in 1979, for example, a passenger with the flu boarded an airplane in Homer, Alaska. The flight was delayed on the ground for three hours, during which the air-recycling rate was turned down to save fuel. The flight itself took another five hours.

CDC researchers who studied the case later found that within three days after the plane landed, 72 percent of the other fifty-three passengers came down with the flu.[2] Health experts say that the risk for spreading disease on airplanes increases on long flights.

In this photo, passengers on Phillippine Airlines protect themselves from a respiratory disease called SARS. This virus became a global threat in 2003.

touching their nose or mouth. The flu is so contagious that it can spread quickly in closed-in spaces, such as classrooms, offices, buses, airplanes, stores, restaurants, and theaters.

Not everybody gets sick when they are exposed to the same sick people, however. Certain things can weaken the body's defenses and make people more vulnerable to germs. For example, the advice children hear growing up, "put a jacket on before you go outside, or you'll catch a cold," isn't exactly true. Colds and flu are caused by viruses, not by the weather. However, exposure to extreme cold may weaken the body's defenses. Then if a person comes into contact with a cold or flu virus, his or her body may be too weak to

> In an average year, flu affects about 10 percent of the American population—more than 25 million people.

fight off the infection. Other factors that may make people more likely to get sick are getting too hot or very tired, not eating very well, or being under a lot of stress.

In an average year, flu affects about 10 percent of the American population—more than 25 million people. More than 110,000 Americans wind up in the hospital every year due to complications from the flu. And each year, the flu is responsible for approximately 36,000 deaths in the United States.[3]

In the Northern Hemisphere, flu season usually starts in November and lasts through March. (In the

Southern Hemisphere, the seasons are reversed: Flu season extends from May through September.) Epidemics tend to peak during winter months because people are crowded indoors more often, giving the virus a better chance to spread. During an epidemic, as much as a quarter of the population gets the flu.

Flu can strike anyone at any age, but since schools are a great place for viruses to run wild, usually families with school-age children are the first to be hit by the flu bug. Unlike colds, not everybody gets the flu every year. In fact, many people may go for years without catching it. Those who do get the flu rarely get it more than once in a year.

Breathing for Life

Flu and pneumonia are diseases of the respiratory system. To understand how they affect the body, you need to know the basics about the respiratory system and how the lungs work in breathing.

All the living cells that make up the human body get energy for their many activities from oxygen (a gas from the air). The cells constantly produce waste products, including a gas called carbon dioxide. The organs that make up the respiratory system work to bring oxygen

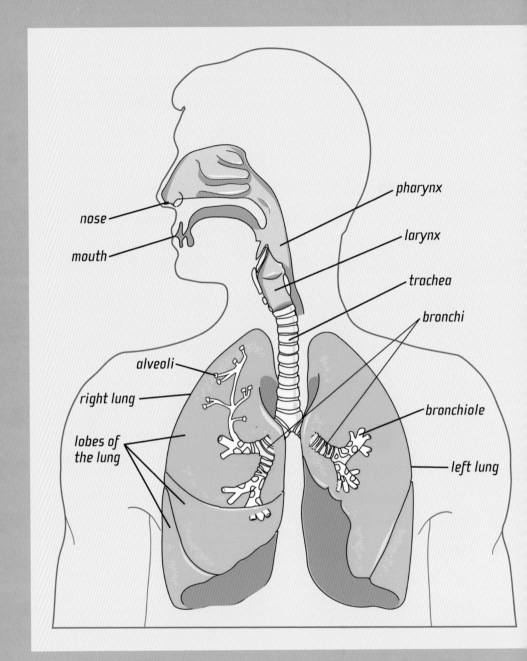

nose

mouth

pharynx

larynx

trachea

bronchi

alveoli

right lung

bronchiole

lobes of
the lung

left lung

Air passes from the mouth or nose to the trachea, bronchia, and eventually to the alveoli, where gases (oxygen and carbon dioxide) are exchanged between blood and air. Flu and pneumonia affect the respiratory system.

from the air into the body and to get rid of carbon dioxide and other waste products.

Your respiratory system looks like an upside-down tree. When you breathe, air is inhaled through your nose and mouth, passes down the throat (pharynx), through the voice box (the larynx), and continues down the main breathing tube, or trachea. Then the air flows through two large tubes (bronchi), which lead into the right and left lungs. The lungs are two large spongy organs that fit snugly on each side of the heart.

Inside the lungs, the bronchi branch into smaller, almost threadlike tubes called bronchioles. They look like the branches of a tree. The bronchioles lead into millions of tiny balloon-like air sacs in the lungs called alveoli. They look like tiny bunches of grapes, but they are too small to see without a microscope. In these alveoli, the exchange of oxygen and carbon dioxide takes place. Oxygen from the breathed-in air passes through the thin outer covering of the alveoli and enters the tiny blood vessels (capillaries) that form a lacy network around them. The blood carries oxygen to the body cells and also picks up the cells' waste products. Carbon dioxide and other wastes pass out of the capillaries and into the alveoli, where they can be breathed out.

Flu Symptoms

When people are hit with the flu, they usually know it. Flu symptoms tend to come on suddenly, and they can really wipe a person out in no time at all. Symptoms develop between one and four days after the person has been exposed to the flu virus. That means that people can spread the disease *before* they even know they have it. They are still contagious for three to four days after their symptoms appear.

If you have several of these symptoms, you probably have the flu:

- high fever (102°F–104°F, lasting 2–3 days)
- headache
- sore throat
- chills
- body aches
- dry cough
- extreme tiredness (fatigue)

The Body Fights Back

The body has many defenses against germs. Viruses that get into the mouth may be swept to the tonsils, where white blood cells, the body's roving disease fighters, are on patrol. The white cells surround germs and gobble

When Is the Flu *Not* the Flu?

When people are throwing up, they tend to say that they have the stomach flu. But this illness is *not* influenza. The two conditions are both caused by viruses, but the viruses that cause them are quite different. The influenza virus attacks the respiratory system. "Stomach" viruses attack the gastrointestinal system—the stomach and intestines. Their main symptoms are vomiting and diarrhea. Influenza rarely causes vomiting, except in young children, who may throw up as a result of high fever. Medical experts do not like the term *stomach flu* because they believe it causes confusion about what flu really is. The stomach virus is actually a milder illness, and its symptoms usually last for only twenty-four hours or so.

them up. Some viruses are swallowed. When they get down into the stomach, the stomach acid kills them.

The nose also has defenses against invading germs. Germs ride on dust particles and drops of liquid, which may be trapped by bristly hairs on the way into the nostrils. The germs that get past these hairs fall into a gooey fluid—mucus—that covers the lining of the nose. Mucus flows along the lining, carrying the trapped germs toward the back of the throat. Some lining cells are equipped with thin hairlike structures called cilia. Millions of them beat back and forth in a wavelike motion, up to one thousand beats a minute, pushing mucus back up to the mouth, where it can be spit out or swallowed. Mucus does not move as fast when the air is cold and dry. Tobacco smoke and alcohol also slow down the rate at which the cilia move mucus along. The longer it takes, the greater the chance viruses have to infect cells along the way. Viruses infect cells most successfully in cold, dry air. In these conditions the mucus that lines the airway passages dries up and are less able to carry off invading viruses.

When cells do become infected, the body's defenses go into a serious battle. The first cells that are attacked release a substance called interferon into the fluids surrounding the cell. Interferon signals neighboring cells, instructing them to make a protein that will fight off viruses. Then when the virus attacks the neighboring cells, the cells are able to disobey the virus's orders, refusing to make more viruses. Interferon helps delay the spread of infection until the body's big guns—the white blood cells—can get to the scene.

An hour or so after a virus invasion, cells give off other chemicals that prompt cells in the nasal lining to produce extra mucus, which helps to trap viruses. Some of the chemicals cause inflammation: swelling, pain,

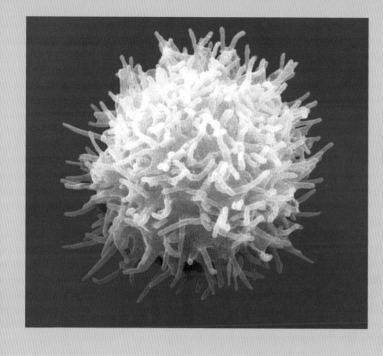

White blood cells begin a body's attack on invading viruses.

heat, and redness around the area of infection. These changes help to slow down virus reproduction and make it easier for white blood cells to move around.

The chemicals released by virus-damaged cells act as distress signals, calling in several kinds of white blood cells. Some gobble up invading germs, destroying them before they can infect cells. Others are able to recognize "foreign" chemicals—those that are not normally found in the body—such as the proteins on the outer coat of a virus. Some white blood cells produce antibodies, proteins that fit onto virus proteins. Antibodies attach to viruses, preventing them from attacking their target cells. Then it is easier for body defenders to destroy the viruses.

Once a person has antibodies that protect against a particular virus, his or her body will be able to prevent future infections by it. The person will have become immune to that disease. Some of these specific antibodies continue to circulate in the blood for years. They are ready to leap into action against attacks by the same type of virus. It generally takes about two weeks to make enough antibodies to fight a virus the body has never met before.

Certain types of white blood cells, called killer T cells, may also fight against viruses. Some of these cells become specialized to recognize and attack that particular kind of virus. These specialized killer T cells multiply, producing an army of defenders that helps fight the infection.

How Do Flu Viruses Work?

The flu virus is covered with a fatty coat containing two types of proteins that stick out in hundreds of spikes. One type of spike is called an H spike from its technical name, hemagglutinin. The H spike matches up with proteins on the surface of respiratory cells, allowing the virus to attach itself to them. N spikes (named from their technical name, neuraminidase) help the virus get into the cells and also help in releasing virus copies from infected cells.

> Once a person has antibodies that protect against a particular virus, his or her body will be able to prevent future infections by it.

Inside the protective coat of a flu virus is a set of hereditary instructions (genes). In the flu virus, the genes are contained in eight short pieces (strands) of genetic material. This is very unusual. In most viruses, all of the genetic material is found in just one long strand. Because flu virus genes are divided among eight separate strands, there is a good chance that they may get shuffled around when the virus reproduces. As a result, the new viruses may not be exact copies of the original. Hence, flu viruses mutate (change) more than other kinds of viruses, producing changes in the spikes in the virus's outer coat.

A person's immune system recognizes a flu virus by these spikes and makes antibodies to match up to the spike proteins. The greater the changes in the flu virus spikes, the less likely it is that the body will be able to use antibodies it has built up from previous infections to stop the new viruses. That is why immunity to influenza is generally not as long lasting as immunity to other diseases, such as chickenpox and polio.

Where Do New Flu Strains Come From?

Scientists believe that new influenza strains develop when an animal or human is infected with two different flu viruses—one that affects only humans and one that affects only animals. The two strains crossbreed or reshuffle, producing new hybrid (combined) viruses that are able to infect humans.

Another theory is that a flu virus becomes so common in humans that it can no longer cause infection because everyone has built up antibodies. It then infects animals, such as ducks or pigs. After a few generations, most people no longer have antibodies against that particular virus, and it returns to attack humans again. This is the "barnyard storage" theory.

The 1957 and 1968 influenza pandemics were traced back to China, and the 1977 Russian flu is also believed to have originated in China. One reason for these similar origins may be that the crossbreeding of animal and human viruses, or barnyard storage, is more likely to occur in a country like China, where many people live in close contact with domesticated animals, such as pigs and ducks.

4

Pneumonia

MANY PEOPLE PROBABLY DO NOT know much about William Henry Harrison, the ninth president of the United States. Harrison did not get a chance to make an impression in history because he contracted pneumonia and died only thirty-one days after being elected into office—the shortest term of any president.

It started on March 4, 1841, when Harrison made his inaugural address on a cold, drizzly, blustery day. He stood outside without any hat or overcoat and delivered a speech that lasted for nearly two hours, the longest inaugural speech of any president. Soon after, he developed a really bad cold, and near the end of the month it

President William Henry Harrison died of pneumonia in 1841, only one month after starting his presidency.

turned into pneumonia. There were no effective treatments at the time, and William Henry Harrison died on April 4, 1841, exactly one month after he took office as president.[1]

In Harrison's time, pneumonia deaths were not uncommon. The disease killed as many as a third of its victims. These days, most pneumonia patients recover after antibiotic treatment. Still, pneumonia kills 5 to 10 percent of the people who get it, and it is one of the leading causes of death in the United States.

In May 1990, people all over the world were shocked when pneumonia took the life of an American icon, Jim Henson, puppeteer and creator of the ever-so-popular Muppets. Almost everyone has heard of Kermit the Frog, Miss Piggy, Oscar the Grouch, Cookie Monster, and other well-known Muppets.

Jim Henson created the Muppets in 1954 when he was only eighteen years old. But it wasn't until 1969 that the Muppets became a nationwide hit when they joined the cast of *Sesame Street*. Henson also produced *The Muppet Show* from 1976 to 1981; it became one of the most popular TV programs in the world.

Henson kept himself so busy doing project after project that sometimes it started to wear him down. In

Jim Henson, creator of the beloved Kermit the Frog, died of an aggressive strain of pneumonia in 1990.

May 1990, after appearing on *The Arsenio Hall Show* in Los Angeles, Henson complained of a sore throat and fatigue. He figured he had the flu and didn't think it was serious enough to see a doctor. By the time he returned home to New York a few days later, Henson felt a lot worse and was having trouble breathing. After Henson's wife, Jane, brought him to the hospital, the medical staff told them that Jim had streptococcal pneumonia. This aggressive form had been attacking his body for three days. Jim was immediately treated with large doses of antibiotics, but the infection had already caused serious damage to his heart and kidneys. Jim Henson died twenty hours later.[2]

How Pneumonia Develops

Pneumonia involves an infection in the lungs. Normally, the body's defenses do a good job protecting the lungs from harmful germs. The cilia and mucus that line the breathing tubes trap particles and move them out of the body. Germs that do manage to get through that first line of defense are killed or held in check by white blood cells, interferon, and other general and specialized defenses.

What Is a Secondary Infection?

In the great flu epidemic of 1918, most of the deaths did not occur directly as a result of the flu. They were due to pneumonia, which developed in the flu patients. Doctors refer to a disease like pneumonia as a secondary infection. It occurs right after another illness or an injury has weakened the body, allowing the *second* illness to develop.

But sometimes problems do develop, especially during a cold or flu infection. Then the body is already vulnerable: The lining of the breathing passages may be inflamed and raw, allowing germs to enter the cells more easily. The body's resources are strained under the load of fighting infection and repairing damage. Typically, during a viral infection like the flu, so much of the body's efforts are concentrated on defense against viruses that the normal defenses against bacteria may be slow to respond.

When a disease-causing agent makes its way into the lungs under these conditions, it settles in the alveoli, and the germs quickly multiply there. Soon inflammation develops, and the alveoli become filled with fluid and pus. Normally the lungs are elastic and can expand as the person inhales and draws in air.

In pneumonia, the inflammation and the buildup of fluids in the alveoli may result in consolidation: The lungs become a fluid-filled mass of tissues that cannot expand and contract with breathing. The exchange of gases cannot take place in the fluid-filled alveoli. As a result, oxygen cannot flow freely to the body cells that need it.

Causes of Pneumonia

Pneumonia may develop for a variety of reasons—actually, there are more than thirty different causes! The germs involved in pneumonia are usually viruses or bacteria, but the disease may also be caused by fungi, or even by chemicals from food, liquid, gases, or dust that were breathed into the lungs.

Bacterial pneumonia: The most dangerous cases of pneumonia are generally caused by bacteria. Streptococcal (or pneumococcal) pneumonia is the most common type of bacterial pneumonia. It is caused by bacteria called *Streptococcus pneumoniae*—the same ones that attacked Jim Henson. These bacteria can be found in the noses and throats of as many as 70 percent of healthy people at one time or another.[3] They can be spread to other people by coughing or sneezing, and normally they do not cause any harm. But when the immune system becomes weakened—possibly by illness, old age, or stress—these bacteria can get past the body's defenses. They can make their way into the lungs, where they can quickly multiply and cause serious problems. Without immediate treatment, the infection

> The germs involved in pneumonia are usually viruses or bacteria, but the disease may also be caused by fungi, or even by chemicals from food, liquid, gases, or dust that were breathed into the lungs.

can also spread through the bloodstream and affect other parts of the body. So much damage may be done that the patient may die.

Symptoms of bacterial pneumonia often start suddenly with a high fever and shaking chills, along with heavy sweating and chattering teeth. Coughing, shortness of breath, rapid breathing, and chest pains are other common symptoms. Coughing may produce rust-colored sputum (mucus and other substances from the lungs, spit out during coughing). People may not realize the seriousness of their condition, confusing these symptoms with the flu and hoping they will just go away.

One type of bacteria, called mycoplasma, often causes a rather mild form of pneumonia. Sore throat and headache are common symptoms, especially in children and adolescents. Chills and fever may also occur. Later, patients may experience violent coughing attacks. Usually there is very little mucus. Mild cases of pneumonia are sometimes called "walking pneumonia" because the symptoms are so mild that people may have it without even knowing it and go on with their normal activities without getting treatment.

Parrot Fever

Parrots are popular pets all over the world, but some pneumonia cases have been caused by bacteria carried mainly by parrots. This has earned the disease the nickname "parrot fever." Psittacosis, or chlamydia pneumonia, is caused by the bacteria *Chlamydia psittaci*. It can spread to people when they are exposed to the dust in bird feathers or to bird droppings, or when they are bitten by an infected bird. The disease is rare; those who are at risk are pet owners, pet shop workers, vets, and other people who regularly handle birds.

Viral pneumonia: As much as 50 percent of all pneumonia cases are caused by viruses. Some of these viruses are the same ones that cause influenza and other respiratory infections. Most cases of viral pneumonia are not very serious and usually go away without any problems. However, bacterial pneumonia may develop in addition, due to the body's weakened defenses.

Symptoms of viral pneumonia start out as flu-like—fever, headache, muscle aches, and dry cough. Around one to three days later, breathing becomes increasingly difficult, and wheezing may occur. The cough becomes worse and produces small amounts of mucus.

Fungal pneumonia: Pneumocystis carinii pneumonia (PCP) is caused by a fungus that infects the lungs of people with weakened immune systems due to illnesses, such as cancer or HIV/AIDS. In fact, PCP is a common problem for AIDS patients. Without preventative medicine, about 40 percent of children with AIDS will develop Pneumocystis carinii pneumonia.[4] Common symptoms are fever; mild, dry cough; shortness of breath; and rapid breathing.

5

Diagnosing and Treating Flu and Pneumonia

I T IS NOT ALWAYS EASY TO TELL if what you have is a cold, the flu, allergies, or something else. These illnesses may share some of the same symptoms, including coughs and headaches, but misdiagnosing the condition could lead to trouble. Amby Burfoot won the Boston marathon in 1968, when he was twenty-two years old. Since then, running has remained an important part of Amby's life. He became the editor of *Runner's World* magazine. He still runs twenty-five miles a week and enters one or two marathons a year.

When Amby was forty, he learned an important lesson. He decided to run in a weekend road race even though he hadn't been feeling well. Cold symptoms had

Ambrose Burfoot crosses the finish line to win the 72nd annual Boston Marathon in 1968. Later in his career he ran a race when he was not feeling well. It turned out he had had the flu and he ended up with a serious case of pneumonia.

Is It a Cold or the Flu?

Symptom	Cold	Flu
fever	rare	high (102°F–104°F, lasts 3–4 days)
headache	rare	usual
aches/pains	slight	usual, often severe
fatigue/weakness	mild	extreme, can last up to 2–3 weeks
runny, stuffy nose	common	sometimes
sneezing	common	sometimes
sore throat	common	sometimes
cough	mild to moderate	common, can become severe

never stopped him from running before. On the morning of the race, Amby had a throbbing headache and sore muscles, symptoms not usually associated with a cold. But still he chose to run. During the race, he became dehydrated and very weak. Two days later, he felt miserable and had hardly any energy to move around. He asked his wife to drive him to the emergency room. Blood tests indicated possible heart and kidney damage, but follow-up tests showed that the first lab results were just due to the effects of severe dehydration. Amby was given intravenous fluids, and his condition improved. He wished he hadn't ignored what his body had been telling him. What he had was not a cold, but the flu, which turned into a serious case of pneumonia.[1]

Normally, exercise is not harmful for people with colds, but it can become very dangerous for people with the flu. Strenuous exercise puts extra strain and stress on the lungs, which may make the condition worse, possibly resulting in pneumonia. Exercise uses a lot of oxygen, but during a lung infection not enough oxygen can get to the body tissues. Other important organs may suffer, too.

Should You See a Doctor?

If you have had the flu before, you can usually recognize flu symptoms right away. Many people do not bother going to the doctor when they have the flu. They just treat themselves at home. In most cases influenza doesn't need medical attention, and patients eventually get better with home remedies.

Normally, exercise is not harmful for people with colds, but it can become very dangerous for people with the flu.

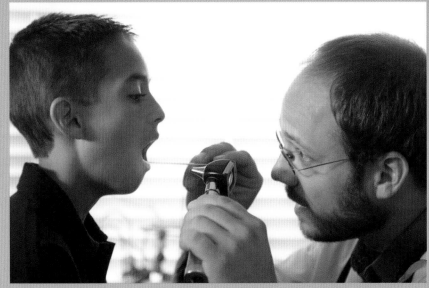

Most cases of the flu are diagnosed by a doctor based on a patient's symptoms.

Sometimes, though, it may be necessary to talk to a doctor, especially if one of the following happens:

- If flu symptoms last more than a week
- If breathing becomes difficult
- If a fever of 103°F or higher develops
- If fever returns after symptoms seem to have been getting better
- If repeated vomiting occurs
- If dizziness occurs, especially when getting out of bed (which could be a sign of dehydration, a loss of fluids from the body tissues)
- If someone with a high risk for complications gets the flu (such as those over the age of 65, or people with chronic health problems, such as asthma, heart disease, diabetes)

Are Tests Necessary?

Until recently, laboratory tests were rarely used to diagnose influenza. Influenza tests were expensive, and results took up to a week to come back. By then, the illness would be almost over. Doctors usually made a diagnosis based on symptoms and whether or not other cases of influenza had been reported in the area. Actually, most cases of influenza are still diagnosed this way. However, there are a number of flu tests available that can produce results in about fifteen minutes, and they cost less than twenty dollars. A growing number of doctors are excited about the use of these tests, but not everybody agrees on whether they are really necessary.

Rapid flu tests, which test samples of fluid from the nose, are designed to detect influenza viruses A and B (although usually they cannot distinguish between the two). The results can help doctors decide whether to prescribe antivirals (drugs to fight the flu infection), antibiotics (drugs to fight bacterial infections), or neither. Dr. William Hueston, a leading researcher at the Medical University of South Carolina in Charleston, argued that the test should not be used routinely for "everyone who comes in with the sniffles. . . . It should be used selectively in patients who are really a diagnostic dilemma and used when it will make a difference in treating the patient."[2]

Pneumonia is a different story. Laboratory tests are usually necessary for diagnosing pneumonia. Pulse oximetry (sometimes called pulse OX) is a fairly simple test to perform. A small probe, which looks somewhat like a clothespin, is carefully attached to the patient's finger, toe, or ear. The device can calculate the amount of oxygen in the bloodstream. If the oxygen level is very low, it indicates poor lung function and could be a sign of pneumonia.

Further tests may include a chest X-ray, which can help to detect if there is a buildup of fluid and which lung is affected. The doctor may also collect samples of sputum and blood and send them to the laboratory to be analyzed. There the sample is mixed with special stains, or dyes, which can reveal the kind of bacterium that is causing the pneumonia. This can help the doctor choose the right kind of antibiotic to prescribe.

Treating With Drugs

Antibiotics do not work on influenza. They kill bacteria, not viruses. Antiviral drugs—drugs that *do* kill viruses—may be prescribed to treat the flu. These drugs help to lessen the severity of the symptoms and make them go away faster. But they have to be taken within the first two days after the symptoms appear to be effective. Relenza (zanamivir) and Tamiflu (oseltamivir phosphate) are common antiviral drugs. Relenza, which can be prescribed for people seven years old and up, is a powder that is inhaled twice a day for five days from a device called a Diskhaler. Tamiflu, which is given to adults and children ages one and older, is available in tablet and liquid form. Like Relenza, it has to be taken twice a day for five days. However, the older antiviral drugs amantadine and rimantadine are much cheaper and work just as well on influenza A—the most common form of flu.

> Antibiotics can be used to treat bacterial pneumonia, but there are no medicines available to treat most types of viral pneumonia.

Antibiotics can be used to treat bacterial pneumonia, but there are no medicines available to treat most types of viral pneumonia. Usually, this kind is not very serious and will go away on its own without any complications. However, some cases of pneumonia are caused by the same virus that causes chickenpox.

These cases can be treated with a number of antivirals (not the same ones that work on flu).

If a person with bacterial pneumonia develops serious breathing problems, hospitalization may be necessary. An important part of the hospital treatment is breathing therapy to increase the amount of oxygen getting into the lungs. A breathing mask delivers oxygen-rich air under pressure to make breathing easier

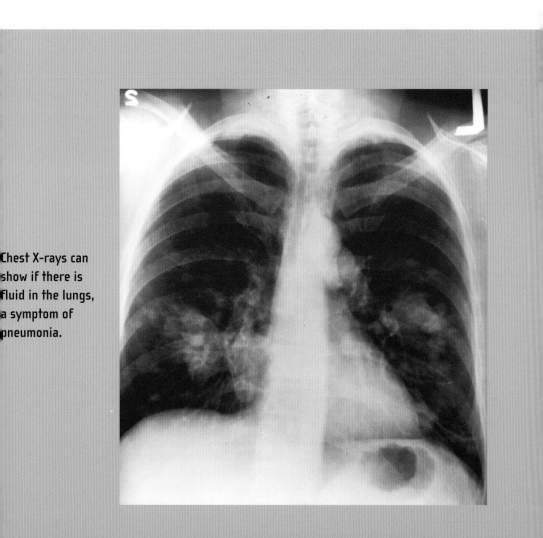

Chest X-rays can show if there is fluid in the lungs, a symptom of pneumonia.

and more effective. Sometimes a plastic tube must be inserted through the nose or mouth down into the trachea, and a machine called a ventilator automatically delivers oxygen-rich air to the lungs.

In a hospital, antibiotics can be given intravenously: They are dripped directly into the patient's bloodstream. That way they can work faster than drugs that are swallowed or inhaled. Sometimes, however, the infection develops so quickly that the damage to the lungs and other organs cannot be repaired even if the drugs wipe out the bacteria. That is what happened to Jim Henson.

When you have the flu, getting rest and drinking lots of fluids can help your recovery.

Aspirin Is Not for Everyone

Children with the flu should not take aspirin. It can lead to Reye's syndrome, a serious or even deadly disease that affects the liver and brain. Doctors used to see cases of Reye's syndrome in some children who took aspirin to treat colds and other viral illnesses. Now that doctors advise parents not to give aspirin to children, Reye's syndrome is very rare.

Home Remedies

Many people treat their flu symptoms at home. While the flu can hit you much harder than the common cold, treatment is basically the same for both: lots of rest, plenty of fluids, and over-the-counter medications for symptoms. Nasal decongestants can unclog a stuffy nose, and acetaminophen and ibuprofen can reduce fever and help relieve aches and pains.

Some medical experts believe that getting extra vitamin C in the diet can make the immune system stronger, helping it fight illnesses better. Oranges are a good source of vitamin C, as are vitamin C tablets. Carrot and tomato juice (or soup), which are rich in vitamin A, may also help boost the immune system.

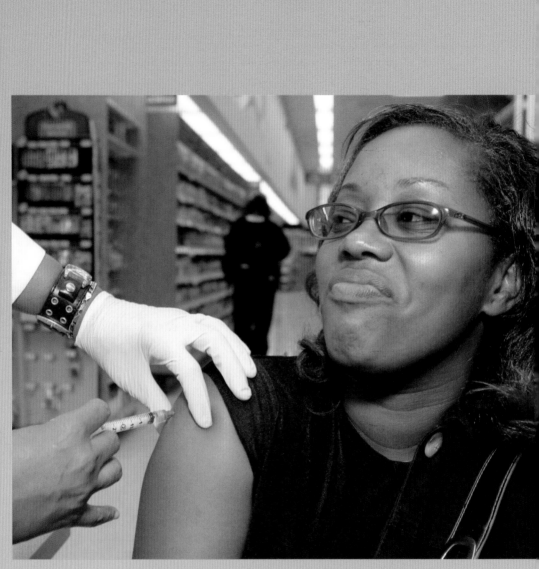

Every year, millions of people get the flu vaccine.

6

Preventing Flu and Pneumonia

WHEN PEOPLE HEARD that the 2003–2004 flu season was off to an unusually early start and there was an especially vicious flu strain on the loose, panic spread through the nation. Normally, epidemics have not yet started to appear by late October or early November, when flu clinics are set up. This time, Texas reported the first flu cases in the beginning of October, and the disease was spreading like wildfire. In fact, some schools in Texas had to close, and emergency rooms were packed with flu victims. Millions of people all over the country rushed to get their flu vaccinations. Nobody wanted to take any chances with that year's flu strain. It was apparently more dangerous than those of past years, killing 93 people in the United States under the age of eighteen and hospitalizing many others between October 2003 and January 2004.

Doctors were afraid that this was going to be the worst flu season in years. When the new deadly strain first appeared, vaccine supplies for the upcoming flu season were already in production. The vaccine did not provide protection specifically against the new strain. However, health experts recommended getting flu vaccinations anyway—they believed that the strains were similar enough that the vaccine would give some protection, which was better than nothing. They turned out to be right: When the 2003–2004 season ended, there had actually been fewer cases than usual, probably because so many people had been vaccinated. Nearly all of the 87 million doses of vaccine prepared for the season were used. (The year before, about 80 million people got the vaccine.)[1]

The Flu Vaccine

The best way to prevent the flu is to get a flu shot. Each year millions of people receive the flu vaccination. Flu vaccines are made up of inactivated or "killed" viruses.

That way the vaccine can trigger the production of antibodies without actually causing symptoms of the disease. People have to get a new flu vaccine each year because flu viruses change each season. (For other viral infections, such as German measles and polio, a single vaccination is good for many years or even a lifetime.)

Each winter, experts from the World Health Organization (WHO), Centers for Disease Control and

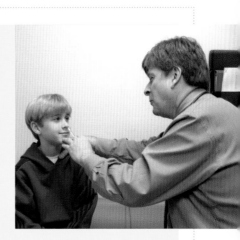

Ouchless Flu Vaccine

Most people do not like getting shots, especially kids. But in 2003, the FDA approved FluMist, a nasal flu vaccine that is sprayed into a person's nostrils. Unlike the injectable flu vaccine, which contains killed virus strains, FluMist is a live attenuated (weakened) vaccine. The viruses are weakened so that they do not reproduce well at body temperature, but the strains are live, so they may cause flu symptoms in some people. Therefore, doctors cannot give the nasal flu vaccine to people with immune problems, such as AIDS or cancer patients, or those with respiratory conditions, such as asthma. Instead, it is acceptable only for healthy people ages five to forty-nine.

Prevention (CDC), the U.S. Food and Drug Administration (FDA), and other medical groups plan the following year's vaccine. They look at the viruses currently circulating in the Northern Hemisphere and those from the previous season in the Southern Hemisphere. The current influenza viruses are combined with older ones, using genetic technology, and grown in fertilized chicken eggs. Then the viruses are

The flu vaccine is safe. The most common complaint is soreness at the injection site, which can last for a couple of days.

inactivated or killed so that they cannot reproduce but will still stimulate the production of antibodies. It takes about two weeks for the body to make antibodies against the influenza virus. These antibodies provide protection for about six months and then become less effective. In 2004, for example, flu vaccines contained killed versions of three different viruses (two strains of influenza A and one influenza B). When the prediction is accurate, up to 70 percent of those vaccinated will not get the flu.

Why do some people get the flu even though they

were vaccinated? Since the vaccine is chosen months in advance, sometimes the virus changes before the flu season starts, and the vaccine will not be effective. However, even if this happens, the vaccine usually makes the illness less severe and reduces the likelihood of the person's developing complications (such as pneumonia). Another possibility is that some people may become infected before the flu vaccine has had a chance to become effective.

The flu vaccine is safe. The most common complaint is soreness at the injection site, which can last for a couple of days. Some people may also have flu-like symptoms, such as low-grade fever, fatigue, and muscle soreness. But these are not signs of flu—the vaccine cannot cause influenza because the viruses it contains are dead. The flu vaccine can be dangerous to some people, though. People who are allergic to eggs should not get a flu shot because the viruses are grown inside chicken eggs.

Who Should Get Flu Shots?

Almost anyone can get a flu shot, but health experts recommend that people who have a high risk for complications should receive the killed, injectable vaccine. They include the following:

- Children 6–23 months old
- Adults over 50 years old
- Pregnant women in their second or third trimester during flu season
- People over two years old with chronic health problems (such as asthma, diabetes, heart disease)
- Healthcare workers who may transmit the disease to high-risk patients, such as those with AIDS or cancer
- Child-care workers in contact with children under 6 months old

In October 2004, just as the annual flu shot clinics were about to begin, British health authorities made a startling announcement. Flu vaccine produced by a British drug company, Chiron Corp., was contaminated with bacteria and would have to be destroyed. Chiron had been expected to produce up to 48 million doses of flu vaccine for the United States—nearly half of the entire supply needed for the 2004–2005 flu season. Another drug company, Aventis-Pasteur, which was already scheduled to provide 54 million doses, agreed to produce an extra 2.6 million. There were also 3 million doses of FluMist, but the total was still far from enough.[2]

Flu-Shot Specials

How about a scenic ferry ride from
Seattle, Washington, to Victoria,
British Columbia—with a flu shot
at its destination? In October
2005, two thousand people paid
$105 each for round-trip tickets
on the Victoria Clipper after being
unable to get a flu shot at home. The
two-and-a-half-hour trip ended at the
ferry terminal, where nurses gave the
injections. Other worried Americans signed up for a trip on
the Flu Bus. A $99 ticket bought a round-trip ride from
Grand Forks, North Dakota, to Winnipeg, Canada, and back,
including a flu shot and lunch at a restaurant in Winnipeg.
Still other Americans headed for the southern border,
seeking flu shots in health clinics and drugstores in Mexico.

Meanwhile, a number of American communities held lotteries
for vaccine doses left over after nursing home patients and
others at high risk had received their shots. People drove for
hours for a chance to get a shot at the drive-through clinics.
In Montgomery County, Maryland, there were 800 doses of
vaccine available—and more than 20 thousand people
bought lottery tickets.[3]

Crowds of people lined up for their shots at the first flu shot clinics in local drugstores and supermarkets. Although the shots were given only to those in high-risk groups, the clinics often ran out of vaccine while people were still waiting. Many elderly people, hearing about the long lines and frustration, did not even try to get a flu shot. After a week or two, the rest of the scheduled flu clinics were cancelled so that vaccine supplies could be saved for residents of nursing homes and others most in need of protection. A few months later, however, more than half of the states had dropped the restrictions on who could get flu shots—they had plenty of vaccine available. In other states, supplies were still short. Health officials estimated that millions of people at risk had not received flu shots. In February 2005, the CDC announced that the number of flu cases was somewhat lower than in previous years but was still rising. Meanwhile, that season's vaccine was expected to be only partly effective against a new flu strain that had

People who have a high risk for complications should receive the killed, injectable vaccine.

appeared in California. The World Health Organization recommended that the new strain be included in the vaccine mix for the 2005–2006 flu season.[4]

What Can *You* Do?

Many people do not get flu shots every year. In fact, when vaccine supplies are low, health experts recommend that healthy people from age five to forty-nine should not receive a flu shot so that there will be enough to protect the high-risk people. There are several things you can do to help reduce your chances of getting the flu even if you do not get a flu shot:

- Avoid crowded places, especially where someone is coughing or sneezing (such as movie theaters, airplanes, malls, etc.)

- Try not to touch or get too close to a friend or family member with the flu.

Wash your hands often to keep them free of germs.

- Wash your hands regularly with soap and water, especially before touching your eyes or nose.

Can you take antiviral drugs to avoid the flu? In 2000, the FDA approved the use of Tamiflu to prevent influenza in adults and children age thirteen and older. Studies have shown that a dose of Tamiflu can greatly reduce the chances of getting the flu when taken daily for forty-two days during a community influenza outbreak. However, there is still a lot researchers do not know about the effects and benefits of Tamiflu. Health experts say that this drug should not be a substitute for flu shots.

If you do get sick, here is what you can do to keep from spreading the flu:

- Stay home so that you do not infect other people.
- Do not shake hands or hug or kiss anyone.
- Cough or sneeze into a tissue and throw it away so that other people will not touch or breathe the germs. (Remember, flu viruses can survive outside the body for a couple of hours.)

Pneumonia Vaccine

A pneumonia vaccine can help to prevent pneumococcal disease, an infection caused by bacteria (*Streptococcus pneumoniae*). The pneumococcal vaccine (Pneumovax 23) is like twenty-three vaccines in one.

It contains twenty-three strains of the most common kinds of bacteria that cause pneumococcal disease. Like the injectable flu vaccine, this pneumonia vaccine contains killed germs and is injected into the skin. Until recently it was believed that one shot was good for a lifetime. However, studies have shown that booster shots may be needed.

The pneumococcal vaccine is recommended for high-risk groups, which include people over the age of sixty-five and people with health problems, such as cancer, AIDS, diabetes, asthma, or heart disease.

The Hib vaccine protects against *Haemophilus influenzae* type B (or Hib disease). The *influenzae* part of Hib does not mean it causes influenza. It was given that name years ago because at the time it was thought to cause the flu. Actually, Hib disease is a serious disease that usually strikes children under five years old. It can cause a number of conditions, most commonly meningitis and pneumonia. In fact, Hib is the leading cause of bacterial meningitis and bacterial pneumonia in children under five.

Since the Hib vaccine was added to babies' routine vaccination schedules in the early 1990s, the rate of Hib disease has dropped more than 95 percent in children

A healthy diet will keep your immune system strong.

under five.[5] Additional booster shots given before the age of two help to increase the protection.

Healthy Living

Do you eat plenty of fruits and vegetables and get enough exercise? Health experts say that a healthy lifestyle can help ward off illnesses, such as flu and pneumonia. Every day the things you do, the foods you eat, and how much sleep you get can affect the way you feel. When you take care of your body, your immune system will be better equipped to fight off invading disease germs.

What kinds of foods do you eat? People need to eat a variety of foods. A balanced diet includes plenty of fruit, vegetables, breads, cereals, and pasta, as well as some meats or beans and dairy products. It is okay to eat candy and cookies sometimes, but it is not a good idea to eat too much junk food. These foods contain a lot of sugars and fats. They can make you feel tired and cranky. It is important to eat meat or beans and other foods with a lot of protein. Proteins provide the building blocks for new tissues. When you get sick or get a cut, your body uses proteins to repair damaged tissues.

Vitamins and minerals are important, too. You need a consistent supply of calcium and phosphorus every day to build strong bones. You

> A healthy lifestyle can help ward off illnesses, such as flu and pneumonia.

can get these minerals by drinking milk or eating cheeses, yogurt, and green leafy vegetables.

Exercise does not have to involve going out and jogging or doing a hundred jumping jacks to get your body into shape. Exercise can be any physical activity that you like to do, such as bike riding, swimming, dancing, or playing basketball or soccer. All these activities help keep your muscles in shape and work your heart and lungs. But how much exercise does a person need to stay healthy? Not everyone agrees. Some experts say that a person needs an hour nearly every day to get the health benefits, but many studies show that twenty to thirty minutes most days is enough to make a difference. These "workouts" do not have to be high-intensity efforts that leave you sweating and huffing. Moderate exercise, such as walking, is fine, and even little changes in lifestyle, like taking the stairs instead of the elevator, or walking to a neighbor's house instead of getting a ride, can help.

Not getting enough sleep can make you tired and cranky all day long. It also lowers your immune defenses and allows disease germs to sneak in. The main repair work in the body goes on while you are sleeping, so missing too much sleep over a long period of time can really wear your body down and make it more vulnerable to illnesses.

7

Flu and Pneumonia and the Future

FOR DECADES, PEOPLE HAVE BEEN trying to uncover the mysteries of the influenza virus that swept through the world in 1918. In the 1950s, a young Swedish pathologist, Johan Hultin, went on an expedition to Brevig Mission, Alaska. There, more than 80 percent of the adult population had died in the 1918 pandemic. In a graveyard there, he dug up bodies of influenza victims, hoping that the virus had been preserved in the ground's permafrost. (Permafrost is a layer of earth that remains frozen and never melts.) Hultin was able to retrieve some frozen tissue samples from the flu victims, but he was unable to isolate the virus because technology was not yet sophisticated enough.

In the 1990s Kirsty Duncan, a Canadian medical geographer and climatologist, became intrigued after reading about the 1918 flu pandemic and the devastating effect it had all over the world. While researching the deadly pandemic, Duncan learned about seven miners who had contracted the Spanish flu and died in October 1918 in Longyearbyen, Norway. If the miners' bodies were buried in the region's permafrost, Duncan thought, then perhaps she could recover preserved tissue samples containing live influenza viruses. In August 1998, Duncan set out for Norway, together with a team of international scientists. It had taken five years of work after she had made her plans public, as she applied for permits, requested permission from local authorities, sought grants to fund the project, and took precautions to make sure that any live viruses they might find would not escape. This half-million-dollar effort was not a total success; the team did obtain tissue samples from the miners, but the bodies had been buried in shallow graves, not in the permafrost, and were badly decomposed.

Ironically, even before Duncan's team set out for Norway, a different research team had begun to report results on the structure of the 1918 flu virus.

This view of the graveyard in Longyearbyen, Norway, shows the area where scientists started to search for secrets of the 1918 flu pandemic. By taking tissue samples of the victims, scientists hoped to find clues about the virus.

When Jeffery Taubenberger, a research pathologist at the Armed Forces Institute of Pathology in Washington, D.C., heard about Kirsty Duncan's plans, he had already been working on his own project, examining viral genes from lung tissue he had retrieved from flu victims in the pathology warehouse.

Taubenberger was concerned about the possible dangers of the live flu virus Kirsty Duncan hoped to find. He thought that his own approach, working with preserved specimens of dead virus, could get results more safely. He wrote up a scientific paper on his work, which was published in the March 1997 issue of *Science* magazine. Johan Hultin read Taubenberger's article in *Science* and realized that methods of analysis had made enormous advances since his own flu studies back in 1951. Now seventy-two, Hultin was retired, but he grew excited at the possibility of getting back into flu research. He wrote to Taubenberger, describing his work and background; he still had contacts in Alaska, he said, and could make another trip to Brevig to get more samples. He'd pay for the trip himself, so they would not need to apply for any federal funds or get tangled up in bureaucratic complications. And he'd be ready to leave the next week!

Quietly, without any publicity, Johan Hultin traveled to Alaska in August 1997. After learning that the graves in Brevig had not been disturbed since his last visit forty-six years before, he persuaded the villagers to give him permission to open the graves again. With the help

A number of scientists, including Taubenberger, believe that another flu pandemic, possibly as dangerous as the one in 1918, is inevitable.

of four young men from the village, he dug into the permafrost at the grave site. Many of the bodies were just skeletons, but on the second day of digging, Hultin found several well-preserved bodies and took samples of lung tissue. He placed slices of tissue, still frozen, in a solution provided by Taubenberger, which would preserve any virus that might be present. He carried the samples back to the United States in an insulated, refrigerated pack, and then shipped them to Taubenberger's lab. The whole trip cost only a few thousand dollars.[1]

Jeffery Taubenberger and his research team used the samples to isolate an important flu virus gene. The gene directs the production of a protein called hemagglutinin that the virus uses to find its way into the lung cells. Hemagglutinin's genetic code has been completely sequenced, but so far, it has not provided the kind of answers scientists are looking for, such as where it came from or how it became so lethal. It did, however, shed light on the origins of the virus and showed that the 1918 flu virus was not related to strains that infected pigs or horses. Instead, it probably came from birds.

The Next Flu Pandemic?

Why are scientists so determined to unlock the mysteries of the 1918 flu virus? What does a virus from last century have to do with today? Taubenberger believes that by studying the genetic makeup of the 1918 virus, scientists may be able to use the information to avoid a possible flu pandemic in the future. A number of scientists, including Taubenberger, believe that another flu pandemic, possibly as dangerous as the one in 1918, is inevitable. In an interview, Taubenberger commented on the possibility: "Just looking at the clinical records of the past hundred years, I think it's extraordinarily likely that another influenza pandemic will occur. . . . they seem to occur with great regularity every 10 to 30 years, and so it has been 30 years since the 1968 [Hong Kong flu] pandemic. So the odds are very great, practically a hundred percent, that another pandemic will occur."[2]

In May 1997, scientists were afraid that a new pandemic had begun when a three-year-old boy died of influenza in Hong Kong. Since most new flu strains originate in China, doctors there were used to sending throat cultures to major research facilities, such as the Centers for Disease Control and Prevention. The results were disturbing: The disease was caused by a strain of avian flu, or "bird flu," which infects chickens and other birds. This deadly flu strain, avian influenza A H5N1, had already killed millions of chickens in Hong Kong, but avian flu does not normally spread to humans. (The unusually deadly strain responsible for the 1918 pandemic was apparently an exception and did jump from birds to humans.)

Efforts to control the spread of the disease included the destruction of 1.5 million chickens. During the outbreak, eighteen people were hospitalized with the avian flu, and six of them died. Scientists confirmed that the avian flu had spread from bird to human, but there was no evidence that it could be transmitted from person to person.

Many birds suspected of having the bird flu virus were destroyed during the bird flu outbreaks in 1997 and 2003.

In the years that followed, scientists were braced for another avian outbreak, but only small numbers of avian flu cases were reported in Hong Kong in 1999 and again in 2003. Outbreaks occurred in other parts of Asia as well, such as Thailand and Vietnam. Fortunately, the outbreaks did not turn into a catastrophic pandemic.

In September 2004, health officials in Thailand reported that the new bird flu (A H5N1) had apparently been transferred from a sick child (who had caught it from chickens) to her mother. This first case of human-to-human transmission suggested that the new strain was evolving closer and closer to a form that could cause epidemics. It was not very contagious yet, but after the news came out, the U.S. government placed an order for 2 million doses of a new vaccine to protect people against it—just in case.[3]

Emerging Diseases

The Asian bird flu was just one example of many new diseases that have been appearing recently, caused by germs that had never been seen before. Because of widespread world travel and commerce, these "emerging diseases" spread more rapidly than epidemics did in the past. A local problem can very quickly become a global problem.

In 2003 a dangerous respiratory illness, called severe acute respiratory syndrome (SARS), became a global threat after it first appeared in southern China in November 2002 and was spread to other parts of the world by travelers. SARS is usually spread by contact with virus-contaminated droplets when an infected person coughs or sneezes. The condition starts off with flu-like symptoms, including high fever, headache, chills, and body aches. Then a persistent dry cough may develop, and in 10 to 20 percent of cases severe breathing difficulties occur, requiring the use of a mechanical breathing device. Many patients develop

In December 2003, people in Taiwan became fearful that a new round of SARS was hitting the island. These two women wear custom-made face masks to protect them from the SARS virus.

pneumonia. Because the disease is so contagious, many health workers who cared for the patients became SARS victims, too. In Asian cities during the outbreak, people started wearing protective face masks whenever they went out.

According to the World Health Organization (WHO), between November 2002 and July 2003, a total of 8,098 cases of SARS were reported worldwide; 774 people died from the disease. In the United States, only eight people were confirmed to have SARS, and none of them died.[4] During the global outbreak, the WHO recommended that travelers avoid taking any unnecessary trips to areas affected by SARS, including Toronto, Singapore, and parts of China.

By July 2003, the SARS outbreak seemed to be under control. Since that time, only a small number of cases were being reported in parts of China, and by early 2005, SARS did not pose a serious threat.

Chances are if a flu strain *does* appear someday with the same potential for global devastation as the one in 1918, the outcome will be completely different. Technology and medical knowledge have become much more advanced than they were a hundred years ago. Scientists have studied influenza for many years, and

Richard J. Webby

SPOTLIGHT
Building a New Flu Vaccine

It is a constant battle to keep up with the ever-changing flu viruses and develop vaccines to protect people from them. Usually scientists can predict the changes, but every once in a while, the virus surprises them—like the avian flu that suddenly jumped from birds to humans. One of the scientists on the front lines of flu vaccine research is Richard J. Webby, a virologist at St. Jude Children's Research Hospital in Memphis, Tennessee. He has developed techniques to isolate key genes from the avian flu virus. He inserts these genes into standard vaccine strains. The new hybrid (combined) viruses can then be used to produce an immune response in a person to the new avian strain without causing the disease. Like other flu researchers, Webby uses ferrets as an animal model. There is one difficulty, though: These animals are so susceptible to human flu that it can be difficult to find ferrets that have not already been exposed.

Developing a new flu vaccine is a long process. It takes at least six months to get one into production. Webby believes that although vaccination techniques will improve and new anti-flu drugs will be developed, "that's not going to get rid of the virus. Flu is here to stay."[5]

now there are medicines that can ward off complications of the flu. While it is possible that a vicious new flu strain could pop up in the future, people are more capable of stopping it from becoming a worldwide disaster.

Questions and Answers

I've got a sore throat, my nose is stuffed up, and I have a terrible cough. Is this just a bad cold, or is it the flu? That depends on what other symptoms you have. Are you running a high fever, are your muscles achy, or have you been having chills and shivering? These are signs of the flu. Are you having severe chest pains or a lot of trouble breathing? If so, you may have pneumonia.

If I get the flu, do I need to see the doctor? Generally, no. Home remedies, such as getting plenty of rest, drinking fluids, and taking over-the-counter medicines to relieve symptoms are usually the only treatment you need. You should see a doctor if a fever lasts for more than two days, if you cannot stop coughing, or if you have severe chest pains or trouble breathing.

I heard you shouldn't take aspirin for the fever and aches that come with the flu. Why not? In children and teenagers, taking aspirin during a cold or flu can lead to Reye's syndrome, a serious or even deadly disease that affects the liver and brain. It's better to take acetaminophen or some other non-aspirin pain reliever.

The flu sounds dangerous. If I get it, will I die? Fortunately, these days that's not very likely. Flu is dangerous mainly to very young children, very old people, people with weakened immune defenses such as

AIDS patients, and those with serious chronic health problems such as asthma, diabetes, or heart disease. The flu strain that swept through the world in 1918, killing millions of healthy young adults, was an exception. If a strain like that appeared today, we have better treatments that could probably save most of the patients.

I'm just getting over the flu and I'm finally starting to feel better. Can I get back to playing basketball? Even though you're feeling better, your body is still recovering from the fight against the germs. Health experts say you should wait a couple more weeks to avoid coming down with any complications, such as a bacterial infection or even pneumonia.

I'm afraid to get a flu shot because I know someone who got the flu right after she got her shot. Flu shots can't give you the flu because the viruses in the vaccine are dead. Your friend may have caught the flu before her body had a chance to use the vaccine to produce protective antibodies. The newer inhaled flu vaccine does contain live viruses, but they are weakened. They may cause some symptoms, but could be dangerous only for people with weakened immune defenses.

Flu and Pneumonia Timeline

412 B.C.   Hippocrates describes an epidemic in Athens that is probably influenza.

A.D. 1600s   Italians call flu "influenza."

1918   Spanish flu pandemic sweeps the world.

1931   Pathologist Richard Shope proves swine flu is caused by a virus.

1933   Influenza type A virus is identified.

1940   Influenza type B virus is identified.

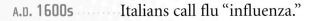

1944   The injectable flu vaccine is first developed.

1947   Influenza type C virus is identified.

1957   Asian flu pandemic sweeps the world.

1968   Hong Kong flu pandemic sweeps the world.

1977   First pneumonia vaccine is approved.

1983   Pneumovax 23 is approved.

1988 An effective Hib (*Haemophilus influenzae* type B) vaccine becomes available.

1997 Asian bird flu spreads to humans.

2003 SARS becomes a global threat; FDA approves the first nasal flu vaccine.

2004 Bacterial contamination causes authorities to order the destruction of millions of doses of flu vaccine; only those at greatest risk of flu complications are allowed to be vaccinated.

For More Information

American Lung Association
1740 Broadway
New York, NY 10019
1-800-LUNG-USA (1-800-586-4872)
<http://www.lungusa.org>

Centers for Disease Control and Prevention
1600 Clifton Road, NE
Atlanta, GA 30333
404-639-3534
1-800-311-3435
<http://www.cdc.gov>

National Institute of Allergy and Infectious Diseases
6610 Rockledge Drive, MSC 6612
Bethesda, MD 20892-6612
<http://www.niaid.nih.gov>

Chapter Notes

Chapter 1. Flu Season

1. Knight Ridder, "Martin Hopes Flu Flees by Game Time," *Charleston Post and Courier,* June 15, 2003, <http://www.charleston.net/stories/061503/spo_15martin_flu.shtml> (October 28, 2004).

2. Tom Canavan, "Ailing Martin Couldn't Help Nets in Game 5," *The Associated Press,* June 14, 2003, <http://www.enquirer.com/editions/2003/06/14/spt_ wwwsptsn-ba1b14.html> (October 28, 2004); Jerry Bembry, "K-Mart Blue but Not Special in Nets' Defeat," *ESPN.com*, June 15, 2003, <http://sports.espn.go.com/nba/playoffs2003/story?id=1568501> (October 28, 2004).

3. "The Influenza (Flu) Viruses," *Centers for Disease Control and Prevention,* January 15, 2004, <http://www.cdc.gov/flu/about/fluviruses.htm> (October 28, 2004).

Chapter 2. Flu's Impact on History

1. "Flu, 1918–1919," Our Fascinating Earth, n.d., <http://www.fascinatingearth.com/Flu,%201918-1919. htm> (June 9, 2004); PBS, *Influenza 1918,* "The First Wave," © 1995–2004, <http://www.pbs.org/wgbh/amex/influenza/peopleevents/pandeAMEX86.html> (March 22, 2004).

2. Wendy Murphy, *Coping with the Common Cold* (Alexandria, Va.: Time-Life Books, 1981), p. 104.

3. Jack Fincher, "America's Deadly Rendezvous with the 'Spanish Lady,'" *Smithsonian,* January 1989, pp. 139, 142.

4. Gina Kolata, *Flu: The Story of the Great Influenza Pandemic of 1918 and the Search for the Virus That Caused It* (New York: Simon & Schuster, 1999), pp. 73–75.

5. Evelyn Zamula, "How to Avoid the Flu," *FDA Consumer,* November 1994, pp. 16–19.

6. National Institute of Allergy and Infectious Diseases (NIAID), "Flu," *Health Matters,* April 2004, <http://www.niaid.nih.gov/factsheets/flu.htm> (October 28, 2004).

Chapter 3. What Is the Flu?

1. Author's personal experience (LSN).

2. "Overview of IAQ Problems in Airplanes," *Aerias, Air Quality Sciences,* 2001, <http://www.aerias.org/kview.asp?DocId=134&spaceid=4&subid=34>; *Washington Post Wire Service,* "Flu Diagnosis Covers Multitude of Woes," *The Star-Ledger* (Newark, N.J.), January 19, 1992, p. H3. (October 28, 2004).

3. The New York City Department of Health and Mental Hygiene, "Who Should Receive the Influenza Vaccine?: Flu Information," *New York City Web Site,* <http://www.nyc.gov/html/imm/imminflu.html> (October 28, 2004).

Chapter 4. Pneumonia

1. Scholastic Library Publishing, "Welcome to the American Presidency," *Grolier Multimedia Encyclopedia,* © 2004, <http://ap.grolier.com/article=atb999b409&templatename=/article/article.html> (October 28, 2004); John Sotos, MD, "Medical History of President William Harrison, © 2000–2004, <http://www.doctorzebra.com/prez/t09.htm> (October 28, 2004).

2. John Culhane, "Unforgettable Jim Henson," *Reader's Digest,* November 1990, pp. 124–129.

3. "Pneumococcal Pneumonia," *National Institute of Allergy and Infectious Diseases,* August 2001, <http://www.niaid.nih.gov/factsheets/pneumonia.htm> (October 28, 2004).

4. "Pneumocystis carinii," *Nemours Foundation,* September 2001, <http://kidshealth.org/PageManager.jsp?dn= KidsHealth&1ic&=1&ps=107&cat_id=20041&article_set=22945> (October 28, 2004).

Chapter 5. Diagnosing and Treating Flu and Pneumonia

1. Jim Thornton, "The Sneeze Factor," *Men's Health,* April 1992, pp. 24–25.

2. Victoria Stagg Elliott, "Flu Testing Is Usually Not Cost-Effective," *AM News,* March 1, 2004, <http://www. ama-assn.org/amednews/2004/03/01/hlsd0301.htm> (October 28, 2004).

Chapter 6. Preventing Flu and Pneumonia

1. Michelle Meadows, "A Look at the 2003–2004 Flu Season," *FDA Consumer Magazine* (March–April issue), <http://www.fda.gov/fdac/features/2004/204_flu.html> (October 28, 2004); Victoria Stagg Elliott, "Flu Season Gets Early Start; Public Health Pushes Vaccine," *amednews.com,* November 10, 2003, <http://www.ama-assn.org/amednews/2003/11/10/hlsa1110.htm> (October 28, 2004).

2. Amanda Spake, "The Flu and You," *U.S. News & World Report,* November 1, 2004, pp. 56-61.

3. Sarah Kershaw and Eli Sanders, "For Inventive Business (and Health) Officials, Flu-Shot Specials," *New York Times,* October 29, 2004, <http://www.nytimes.com/2004/10/29/health/29vaccine. html> (March 5, 2005).

4. Associated Press, "CDC: 'Don't waste' flu vaccine," *CNN.com Colds & Flu Report,* February 11, 2005, <http://www.cnn.com/2005/HEALTH/02/11/flu.shots.ap/> (March 4, 2005).

5. CDC, "*Haemophilus influenzae* Serotype b (Hib) Disease," December 2003, <http://www.cdc.gov/ncidod/dbmd/diseaseinfo/haeminfluserob_t.htm> (October 28, 2004).

Chapter 7. Flu and Pneumonia and the Future

1. Gina Kolata, *Flu: The Story of the Great Influenza Pandemic of 1918 and the Search for the Virus That Caused It* (New York: Simon & Schuster, 1999), pp. 255–266.

2. "Jeffery Taubenberger On: New Flu Due?" <http://www.pbs.org/wgbh/amex/influenza/sfeature/drjeffrey18.html> (May 21, 2004).

3. Brenda Mackenzie, "Bird Flu Goes Human-to-Human," *New Scientist,* October 2, 2004, pp. 10–11.

4. Centers for Disease Control and Prevention, "Frequently Asked Questions About SARS," April 26, 2004, <http://www.cdc.gov/ncidod/sars/faq.htm> (October 28, 2004).

5. Lisa Stein and Nell Boyce, "On the Tail of Bird Flu," *U.S. News & World Report,* February 16, 2004, p. 15.

Glossary

alveoli (sing. alveolus)—The tiny air sacs in the lungs, where gas exchange takes place.

antibiotics—Medicine that kills bacteria.

antibodies—Proteins produced to attach specifically to surface chemicals on an invading virus.

antiviral drugs—Medicine that kills viruses.

attenuated—Weakened; made less toxic or deadly.

bronchi (*sing.* bronchus)—The two large air tubes leading from the trachea into the lungs.

bronchioles—Smaller air tubes of the lungs, which branch off from the bronchi.

bronchitis—Infection of the larger air passages in the lungs.

cilia—Tiny hairlike structures on the cells in the membrane that lines the respiratory passages; cilia beat back and forth to create an upward current in the mucus.

consolidation—A condition in which the lungs become a hardened mass of tissues that cannot expand and contract (get smaller) with breathing.

epidemic—An infectious disease that spreads over a wide area.

hemagglutinin—A surface protein on the flu virus that combines with red blood cells and causes them to clump together.

host—A living plant or animal that provides food and shelter for another creature.

immune—Protected against a certain disease.

immune system—The body's disease-fighting system, which includes the white blood cells, interferon, and many other chemicals.

inflammation—Swelling, pain, heat, and redness in the tissues around a site of infection.

influenza—Also known as the flu; a contagious viral disease that produces such symptoms as a high fever, muscle aches and pains, headache, sore throat, and cough.

interferon—A protein released by virus-infected cells that protects other cells from infection.

killed vaccine—A vaccine made from viruses that have been killed by heat or chemicals.

killer T cells—A type of white blood cells that attack and kill invading germs.

larynx—The voice box.

live virus vaccine—A vaccine made from weakened live viruses, capable of infecting humans but not of causing disease.

mutation—A change in form or nature.

mycoplasma—The smallest and simplest bacterium, which lacks the tough outer covering (cell wall) typical of other bacteria.

neuraminidase—A surface protein on the flu virus that helps the virus enter healthy cells and helps infected cells release the virus copies.

nucleic acids—Chemicals that carry genetic information for producing new cells and directing the cell's activities.

pandemic—An infectious disease that spreads all around the world, involving millions of people.

pharynx—Throat.

pneumonia—A serious illness that causes inflammation of lung tissue, resulting in sharp chest pain, severe cough, and very high fever; can be caused by viruses, bacteria, or inhaled chemicals.

Reye's syndrome—A rare but serious illness associated with taking aspirin during a viral infection.

sputum—Mucus or pus expelled from the lungs by coughing.

trachea—The windpipe; the breathing tube that connects the throat to the bronchi.

ventilator—A machine that automatically delivers oxygen-rich air to the lungs when a person is unable to breathe without help.

Further Reading

Books

Aronson, Virginia. *The Influenza Pandemic of 1918.* Philadelphia: Chelsea House, 2000.

Emmeluth, Donald. *Influenza.* Philadelphia: Chelsea House, 2003.

Getz, David. *Purple Death: The Mysterious Flu of 1918.* New York: Henry Holt & Company, Inc., 2000.

Isle, Mick. *Everything You Need to Know About Colds and Flu.* New York: Rosen Publishing Group, 2000.

Kolata, Gina. *Flu: The Story of the Influenza Pandemic of 1918 and the Search for the Virus That Caused It.* New York: Simon & Schuster, 1999.

Monroe, Judy. *Influenza and Other Viruses.* Mankato, Minn.: LifeMatters, 2002.

Internet Addresses
(See also **For More Information.**)

Centers for Disease Control and Prevention. *Influenza (Flu).* <http://www.cdc.gov/flu/index.htm>.

PBS Online. *American Experience.* "Influenza, 1918." <http://www.pbs.org/wgbh/amex/influenza/>.

Index

DATE DUE

22586

F
Hol

Holt, Kimberly Willis
My Louisiana sky

$13.99